# WIN

# AN IRS

# TAX AUDIT

## One Hour Crash Course in
## How to Prevail at an
## IRS Tax audit

**Brent J. Jordan, Esq., LL.M.**

# Table of Contents

## Chapter 1
## Introduction

## Chapter 2
## Taxpayer Legal Rights

## Chapter 3
## Tax Professionals

# Chapter 4
# IRS Employees.........................23

# Chapter 5
# IRS Tax Audit.........................31

# Chapter 6
# IRS Tax Appeal........................55

# Other Books by
# Brent J. Jordan, Esq. LL.M.........67

# CHAPTER 1

# Introduction

I have a legal insight about IRS tax Audits, "The more you know, the less you owe."

You might respond by saying: "I can't possibly learn this win an IRS tax audit. It's way too complicated. I need a Tax Attorney or an Accountant CPA to stand up to the IRS." Not so fast. With this one hour crash course in IRS tax audits, you may be just as capable of handling a routine IRS tax audit yourself, all alone, or with a little assistance from a tax professional, and thus save more of your hard earned money. You'll also become more confident and relaxed once the great big mystery of a tax audit is revealed to you.

And besides, the IRS will be using tax jargon and lingo to intimidate you into turning over your hard earned money. You therefore need to become familiar with this jargon and lingo if you want to prevail at your IRS audit. So let's get started.

The success or failure of all IRS tax audits begin and end with your properly reporting and documenting all your income, exemptions, adjustments, deductions, and credits on your Federal income tax return. I call this "Audit Proofing." In other words, you must take affirmative steps to bullet proof your income tax returns to reduce your chances of being chosen for an IRS audit, and in the unlikely event you are chosen, reducing your chances of having to pay more taxes to the IRS than you legally owe.

The key to Audit Proofing is "Documentation." Without proper documentation, you end up in the IRS tax cemetery where the IRS picks your bones clean. To avoid this tragedy, you must maintain written records that are accurate and complete, and which support your Federal income tax returns. We discussed all about how to audit proof your proactive tax plan in Chapter 5.

Always remember one important fact about an IRS tax audit. You are not presumed innocent until proven guilty when it comes to the IRS. Just the opposite is true. When it comes to an IRS tax audit, you are presumed guilty until you prove your innocence. It's hard to believe our 5th amendment rights to the U.S. Constitution have been tossed straight into the garage when it comes to an IRS tax audit. But it doesn't matter what we believe. This is fundamental truth of our U.S. tax system. This is the cold hard painful realty of an IRS tax audit. So we must learn to live with it, and with proper documentation, you can avoid a "walletectomy." Translation? The surgical removal of your hard earned money from your wallet by an IRS Tax Auditor.

# CHAPTER 2

# Taxpayer Legal Rights

In the event you are selected for an IRS tax audit, you should first become familiar with your legal rights. Taxpayer's legal rights that will assist you with your IRS tax audit consist of the IRS Taxpayer Bill of Rights, Freedom of Information Act, and court subpoenas.

IRS laws that empower your legal rights are found in the Internal Revenue Code, U.S. Treasury Regulations, U.S. Tax Court published opinions, IRS Revenue Procedures, IRS Private Letter Rulings, IRS Publications, IRS Manuals, and IRS Tax Forms.

### IRS Taxpayer Bill of Rights

The IRS issued a Taxpayer Bill of Rights. I call it the 10 commandments. Here is the Taxpayer Bill of Rights exactly as written by the IRS:

(1) <u>The Right to Be Informed</u>

Taxpayers have the right to know what they need to do to comply with the tax laws. They are entitled to clear explanations of the laws and IRS procedures in all tax forms, instructions, publications, notices, and correspondence. They have the right to be informed of IRS decisions about their tax accounts and to receive clear explanations of the outcomes.

(2) <u>The Right to Quality Service</u>

Taxpayers have the right to receive prompt, courteous, and professional assistance in their dealings with the IRS, to be spoken to in a way they can easily understand, to receive clear and easily understandable communications from the IRS, and to speak to a supervisor about inadequate service.

(3) <u>The Right to Pay No More than the Correct Amount of Tax</u>

Taxpayers have the right to pay only the amount of tax legally due, including interest and penalties, and to have the IRS apply all tax payments properly.

(4) <u>The Right to Challenge the IRS's Position and Be Heard</u>

Taxpayers have the right to raise objections and provide additional documentation in response to formal IRS actions or proposed actions, to expect that the IRS will consider their timely objections and documentation promptly and fairly, and to receive a response if the IRS does not agree with their position.

## (5) The Right to Appeal an IRS Decision in an Independent Forum

Taxpayers are entitled to a fair and impartial administrative appeal of most IRS decisions, including many penalties, and have the right to receive a written response regarding the Office of Appeals' decision. Taxpayers generally have the right to take their cases to court.

## (6) The Right to Finality

Taxpayers have the right to know the maximum amount of time they have to challenge the IRS's position as well as the maximum amount of time the IRS has to audit a particular tax year or collect a tax debt. Taxpayers have the right to know when the IRS has finished an audit.

## (7) The Right to Privacy

Taxpayers have the right to expect that any IRS inquiry, examination, or enforcement action will comply with the law and be no more intrusive than necessary, and will respect all due process rights, including search and seizure protections and will provide, where applicable, a collection due process hearing.

## (8) The Right to Confidentiality

Taxpayers have the right to expect that any information they provide to the IRS will not be disclosed unless authorized by the taxpayer or by law. Taxpayers have the right to expect appropriate action will be taken against employees, return preparers, and others who wrongfully use or disclose taxpayer return information.

(9) <u>The Right to Retain Representation</u>

Taxpayers have the right to retain an authorized representative of their choice to represent them in their dealings with the IRS. Taxpayers have the right to seek assistance from a Low Income Taxpayer Clinic if they cannot afford representation.

(10) <u>The Right to a Fair and Just Tax System</u>

Taxpayers have the right to expect the tax system to consider facts and circumstances that might affect their underlying liabilities, ability to pay, or ability to provide information timely. Taxpayers have the right to receive assistance from the Taxpayer Advocate Service if they are experiencing financial difficulty or if the IRS has not resolved their tax issues properly and timely through its normal channels.

**Freedom of Information Act**

The U.S. Freedom of Information Act, found in Section 5 of Chapter 5 of the United States Code, is a law ensuring your public access to U.S. government records. This act carries a presumption of disclosure, and the burden is on the government, not the public, to substantiate why information cannot be released. Upon written request, agencies of the United States government are required to disclose their records, unless they can be lawfully withheld from disclosure under one of nine exemptions listed in the statute. Your right of access is enforceable in a U.S. Federal court.

Here are the opening paragraphs of the Freedom of Information Act:

"Section 552: Public information; agency rules, opinions, orders, records, and proceedings

(a) Each agency shall make available to the public information as follows:

(1) Each agency shall separately state and currently publish in the Federal Register for the guidance of the public-

(A) Descriptions of its central and field organization and the established places at which, the employees (and in the case of a uniformed service, the members) from whom, and the methods whereby, the public may obtain information, make submittals or requests, or obtain decisions;

(B) Statements of the general course and method by which its functions are channeled and determined, including the nature and requirements of all formal and informal procedures available;

(C) Rules of procedure, descriptions of forms available or the places at which forms may be obtained, and instructions as to the scope and contents of all papers, reports, or examinations;

(D) Substantive rules of general applicability adopted as authorized by law, and statements of general policy or interpretations of general applicability formulated and adopted by the agency; and

(E) Each amendment, revision, or repeal of the foregoing.

(2) Each agency, in accordance with published rules, shall make available for public inspection and copying—

(A) Final opinions, including concurring and dissenting opinions, as well as orders, made in the adjudication of cases;

(B) Those statements of policy and interpretations which have been adopted by the agency and are not published in the Federal Register;

(C) Administrative staff manuals and instructions to staff that affect a member of the public;

(D) Copies of all records, regardless of form or format, which have been released to any person under paragraph (3) and which, because of the nature of their subject matter, the agency determines have become or are likely to become the subject of subsequent requests for substantially the same records; and

(E) A general index of the records referred to under subparagraph

(D) Unless the materials are promptly published and copies offered for sale."

You will be very wise to remember this law. You may someday require its tremendous power to secure your taxpayer rights, and to prevail in an IRS tax audit.

## Court Subpoena

You and the IRS can go to a U.S. Court and obtain a Court Subpoena to serve upon any individual or business. A subpoena orders someone to appear, or to produce documents, or both, at a specified time, date, and place.

Court Subpoenas are normally used to obtain documents relevant to an IRS Tax Audit when the IRS or taxpayer is unable to secure documents by other available means. If an individual disobeys a court subpoena, the individual can be forced to appear in front of a court judge who will decide the issue.

# CHAPTER 3

# Tax Professionals

In the event you're chosen for an IRS tax audit, the first decision you must make is deciding whether to handle the audit yourself or hire a Tax Professional. In order to make a wise decision, you need to decide exactly what you want to accomplish, and what monetary and personal price you're willing to pay to make it happen.

**Deciding Who Will Handle Audit**

To help you make an intelligent and informed decision regarding who will handle your IRS tax audit, you should consider three key factors:

(1) <u>Tax Issue</u>

Does the tax matter involve a correspondence audit, office audit, or field audit, or an appeal?

A "correspondence" audit involves an IRS letter sent to your residential home, requesting payment of money for alleged underpayment of taxes in connection with a single

14

tax matter. You can usually handle a correspondence audit yourself or contact a Tax Professional to discuss the content of the correspondence and your legal options, and then handle it yourself.

An "office" audit requires your attendance at an IRS office to discuss no more than four tax matters with an IRS Tax Auditor. In such an event, you can handle it yourself for most tax matters, or contact a Tax Professional to discuss the parameters of the IRS audit and your legal options, and then handle it yourself.

A "field" audit requires an IRS Revenue Agent to come to your business office to investigate and discuss one or more tax matters. You should not handle a field audit yourself. Instead, you should contact a Tax Professional to discuss the parameters of the IRS audit and your legal options and hire the Tax Professional to handle your tax audit.

(2) Economics

Once again, does the tax matter involve a correspondence audit, office audit, field audit, or an appeal?

An IRS "correspondence" audit should not cost more than one hour of advice from a Tax Professional.

An IRS "office" audit normally requires someone to visit an IRS office for one to four hours. You can bring any one of the following persons with you to an office audit: Attorney, Accountant, Enrolled Agent, Tax Preparer, Business Partner, Employee, Spouse, Friend, or any combination thereof. I would recommend against your bringing an entourage of people with you to the audit. One Tax Professional, and one additional person for moral support, should be fine.

An IRS "field" audit at your business office normally takes several days. One Tax Professional is all the people you need for this audit.

In the event you disagree with the final tax assessment rendered by the IRS after your tax audit, you must then decide whether to pay the tax assessment or challenge it. If you decide to challenge the tax assessment, you can choose one of two tax forums where your challenge will be heard. You can file an appeal with the IRS Office of Appeals, or you can file an appeal with a U.S. Court.

If you file an appeal with the IRS Office of Appeals, you will find the legal atmosphere similar to an IRS office audit. Your appeal normally requires someone to visit an IRS Office of Appeals for one to two hours. You can bring any person identified in the IRS office audit.

You can also file an appeal with a U.S. Court, including the U.S. Tax Court, U.S. Court of Appeals, U.S. District Court, or Bankruptcy Court. Now you're talking about much more time; much more competency; and much more money. You can go "in pro per" by yourself; you can retain an attorney to go with you; or you can retain an attorney to go alone. You cannot retain any other individual to go alone. As you can imagine, the legal cost of pursuing one or more of these court appeals is very costly if you decide to hire a Tax Attorney. Be prepared to spend thousands of dollars on legal services and costs.

If you still disagree with the decision of a U.S. Court, you can file a discretionary tax appeal with the U.S. Supreme Court. Your chances of having your tax matter heard before the U.S. Supreme Court are less than winning the Lottery. But who knows? Maybe you'll create a landmark case decision for the entire world to remember you by.

(3) Personal Stress

Once again, does the tax matter involve a correspondence audit, office audit, field audit, or appeal?

As a business owner, you know all about stress. It comes with the territory. It goes hand in hand with success. One famous motivational speaker once said that individuals who succeed in life do not have fewer problems than individuals who fail in life. The only people without problems are those in cemeteries.

You may not be able to control what problems in this world will confront you, including an IRS tax audit, but you can control how you think, feel, and act when those problems confront you. In other words, there is no stress in the world. There is only stress in you, and only when you choose to feel it. You know your stress level. When it comes to an IRS tax audit, if you feel yourself making tax decisions because of your emotional and physical stress, and not because of your calm and rational mind, it's probably time to retain a Tax Professional.

**Attorney**

If you decide to retain an attorney for an IRS tax audit, your best choice is an attorney who specializes in taxation, and who possesses an attorney's master's degree in Federal taxation, otherwise known as an "LL.M" degree.

Retain a tax attorney who is confidant when speaking; aggressive when taking action; and definitely an attorney who has experience with IRS tax audits and the U.S. tax courts.

To make sure your tax attorney's legal fees and costs remain under control, here are a few valuable tips: If you like the tax attorney, but not the retainer or hourly fee, ask for a lower fee. Also, obtain a written agreement and itemized monthly billing. Finally, if you disagree with an invoice, call the attorney and ask the attorney to adjust the bill.

**Accountant**

If you decide to retain an accountant for an IRS tax audit, instead of any attorney, your best choice is a licensed Certified Public Accountant (CPA) who is also an Enrolled Agent. If not an Enrolled Agent, than the CPA must have experience handling IRS tax audits on behalf of clients.

Why not any CPA? Because many CPAs limit their work to bookkeeping, payroll taxes, and income tax preparation. In fact, only 5% of the written licensing examination required to become a CPA includes taxation. The remaining 95% is dedicated to income tax preparation.

There is only one good reason for hiring a CPA instead of a tax attorney. A CPA normally charges a lower hourly fee.

All the important factors I provided you regarding a competent Tax Attorney, as well as how to control your fees and costs, apply equally to a CPA.

**Enrolled Agent**

An Enrolled Agent is a federally authorized tax practitioner who has technical expertise in the field of taxation, and who is licensed and empowered by the U.S. Department of the Treasury to represent taxpayers before all administrative levels of the IRS, including examination, collection, and appeals. In addition to taxpayer representation, Enrolled Agents often provide tax consultation services and prepare a wide range of Federal and State tax returns.

Here is what the IRS says about Enrolled Agents:

"An enrolled agent is a person who has earned the privilege of representing taxpayers before the Internal Revenue Service by passing a three-part comprehensive IRS test covering individual and business tax returns, or through experience as a former IRS employee. Enrolled agent status is the highest credential the IRS awards. Individuals who obtain this elite status must adhere to ethical standards and complete 72 hours of continuing education courses every three years. Enrolled agents, like attorneys and certified public accountants (CPAs), have unlimited practice rights. This means they are unrestricted as to which taxpayers they can represent, what types of tax matters they can handle, and which IRS offices they can represent clients before."

Basically, there are two ways to become an Enrolled Agent: Work for the IRS for five years in a position requiring the interpretation of the tax code; or pass all three parts of the Special Enrollment Exam. The exam covers Individuals, Businesses, and IRS Representation, Practices, and Procedures.

Let me make one fact perfectly clear. An Enrolled Agent is not a licensed Accountant, CPA, or Tax Attorney. An Enrolled Agent is normally an experienced income tax preparer who may or may not have worked for the IRS. Retaining an Enrolled Agent who worked for the IRS is clearly the better choice.

There is only one good reason for hiring Enrolled Agent instead of a competent Tax Attorney or CPA. An Enrolled Agent normally charges a lower hourly fee.

All the important factors I have provided you regarding a competent Tax Attorney, as well as how to control your fees and costs, apply equally to an Enrolled Agent.

## Registered Tax Return Preparer

The IRS permits the following individuals to sign a Federal income tax return on behalf of a U.S. taxpayer: Tax Attorney, Certified Public Accountant, Enrolled Agent, and a Registered Tax Return Preparer.

Under current Federal law, a Tax Preparer who possesses a valid "Preparer Tax Identification Number" can prepare, assist, and sign a Federal tax return on behalf of a U.S. taxpayer. A Tax Preparer cannot represent you before the IRS or in a U.S. Court. However, when you represent yourself "in pro per" before the IRS or in a U.S. Court, you can bring a Tax Preparer with you to an IRS tax audit or U.S. Court hearing.

During the past several years, the IRS observed a growing problem with poorly completed Federal tax returns by Registered Tax Return Preparers who were not Enrolled Agents, Certified Public Accountants, or Tax Attorneys. As a result, the IRS launched new efforts to solve this growing problem by trying to impose new regulations for Registered Tax Return Preparers. The IRS only wants individuals who meet the IRS regulations to prepare, assist, and sign Federal tax returns on behalf of U.S Taxpayers.

The IRS calls this new program the "IRS Return Preparer Program." This program seeks to better regulate Tax Preparers who do not possess a CPA or attorney license. To participate in the program, a Tax Preparer must register with the IRS, possess a valid tax preparer tax identification number, and complete a specific amount of hours each year pertaining to Federal tax laws and procedures.

The IRS program has not withstood judicial scrutiny. A U.S. District Court struck down the IRS regulation efforts. The court ruled that Congress never gave the IRS authority to license Tax Preparers.

In any event, to insure a more competent Federal tax return, and to avoid any unqualified or unscrupulous Tax Preparers, you should only retain a licensed Enrolled Agent, CPA, or Tax Attorney to prepare, assist, and sign your Federal Income tax return.

I only recommend you bring along a Registered Tax Return Preparers to an IRS tax audit if you cannot afford a Tax Attorney, CPA or Accountant, or an Enrolled Agent, and you do not want to attend the IRS audit alone.

## Other Helpful People

The IRS allows you to bring almost anyone you want to an IRS audit. Besides a Tax Attorney, CPA, Enrolled Agent, or Registered Tax Return Preparers, you might consider bringing along your bookkeeper, business partner, employee, spouse, or even your best friend, if only for moral support, or to help you handle your stress.

You should seriously consider bringing along one of the forgoing individuals when you handle an IRS tax audit yourself, and this individual can assist you with documentation issues. In the event your audit involves a Federal marital joint income tax return, the IRS permits you to bring your spouse to the IRS tax audit, or your spouse can go without you, or you can go alone.

# CHAPTER 4

# IRS Employees

Now it's time to meet all the IRS employees you might encounter during your IRS tax audit. These individuals include IRS employees you can call by telephone at the IRS Customer Service Center and IRS Taxpayer Assistance Center. These individuals also include various IRS employees you may meet during your IRS tax audit, including an IRS Tax Auditor, Revenue Agent, Special Agent, Appeals Officer, Attorney, and Manager.

## IRS Customer Service Center

The IRS provides all U.S. citizens access to IRS Customer Service Centers located in all 50 U.S. States. You can most likely find a service center in your local area.

The IRS issues this invitation:

"Contact the IRS if you have tax questions such as how to respond to an IRS notice or how to resolve tax problems or how to eliminate tax debt or to look up your tax refund status. When calling, you may ask questions to help you prepare your tax return or ask about a notice you have received. Please be aware that when you conclude your discussion, our system will not permit you to return to your original responder."

The best thing to say about the IRS customer service center is that it's a FREE telephone service. On the other hand, you will not speak with a Tax Professional or IRS Tax Agent or Revenue Agent, and you can only discuss your tax matter over the telephone and not in person. As one Tax Professional commented: "I once conducted a study of the CCS program by asking a CCS employee to provide me answers to 27 tax questions. Only 4 answers were correct." One word of caution. Your reliance upon any verbal tax information given to you by a CSS employee will not constitute a legal defense at your IRS tax audit. As the well-known saying goes: "What is free tax advice worth? The money you paid for it."

**IRS Taxpayer Assistance Center**

The IRS provides all U.S. citizens access IRS Taxpayer Assistance Centers located in all 50 U.S. States. Each U.S. State has at least one office.

The IRS issues this invitation:

"The Taxpayer Assistant Service is an independent organization within the IRS and is *your voice at the IRS*. Our job is to ensure that every taxpayer is treated fairly, and that you know and understand your rights as a taxpayer. We offer free help to guide you through the often-confusing process of resolving tax problems that you haven't been able to solve on your own. Remember, the worst thing you can do is nothing.

The IRS Taxpayer Assistance Center can help you in one of the following situations: First, you have been unable to resolve your tax problem with the IRS, and your tax problem is causing financial difficulties for you, your family, or your business. Second, you or your business is facing an immediate threat of adverse action. Third, you've tried repeatedly to contact the IRS, but no one has responded to you. Finally, the IRS hasn't responded by the date the IRS promised to contact you."

As a general rule, Tax Professionals recommend that you contact the IRS Taxpayer Assistance Center only after you have written the IRS three times, and the IRS failed to contact within 30 days of your last correspondence.

Each state has at least one Local office. Each office is independent of the local IRS office, and reports directly to the National Taxpayer Advocate.

The best thing to say about the IRS Taxpayer Assistant Center is that it's a FREE service, and unlike the IRS Customer Service Centers, you can speak with an IRS employee in person, instead of only over the telephone. On the other hand, you will not speak with a Tax Professional or IRS Tax Agent or Revenue Agent. Nevertheless, you can speak with an IRS employee who normally possesses more tax knowledge and experience than the IRS employees working at IRS Customer Service Centers.

One word of caution: Your reliance upon any verbal tax information given to you by a TAC will not constitute a legal defense. As the saying goes: "What is verbal tax advice worth? The paper it's printed on." This rule is subject to one loophole. You can normally avoid a tax penalty, but not a tax assessment, if you rely upon verbal tax information given to you by an IRS Taxpayer Assistant Center employee, when you obtain and write down the name and badge number of the employee, along with the date, time, tax question you asked, and tax answer given by the employee.

**IRS Tax Auditor**

An IRS Tax Auditor is the IRS employee you meet when you undergo an IRS office audit at an IRS office.

The IRS requires an IRS Tax Auditor to possess a four-year college bachelor's degree, but the degree can be in any subject matter. In other words, there is no requirement that an IRS Tax Auditor possess an accounting degree; a certificate from a commercial tax preparation service, such as H&R Block or Jackson Hewitt; or any accounting classes or experience.

An IRS Tax Auditor receives his tax education and training from the IRS and conducts tax audits according to the IRS way of business.

**IRS Revenue Agent**

An IRS Revenue Agent is the IRS employee you meet when you undergo an IRS field audit at your business office.

The IRS requires an IRS Revenue Agent to possess a four-year college bachelor's degree, but just like an IRS Tax Auditor, the degree can be in any subject matter. Thus, a four-year college degree in History, Philosophy, or English is sufficient. In addition, the IRS requires an IRS Revenue Agent to possess at least 24 semesters of accounting experience or equivalent experience, but there is no requirement that an IRS Revenue Agent possess a certificate from a commercial tax preparation service, such as H&R Block or Jackson Hewitt.

An IRS Tax Auditor also learns how to conduct tax audits according to the IRS way of business.

**IRS Special Agent**

An IRS Special Agent is the IRS employee you meet when you undergo an IRS criminal investigation. An IRS Special Agent is a forensic accountant who "tracks the money," searching for evidence of criminal tax conduct that violates the Internal Revenue Code and other tax laws and regulations. Such crimes normally involve tax evasion, tax fraud, money laundering, and violations of the Bank Secrecy Act Laws.

The IRS has very stringent educational, work experience, and physical and mental requirements for an individual to become an IRS Special Agent. For example, a Special Agent must be more than 37 years old; must submit to a comprehensive mental and physical medical examination; must be willing to work anywhere in the United States; and must possess a license to carry a firearm!

The tax reduction strategies taught in this course will never get an IRS Special Agent snooping around your business. This study course teaches "tax avoidance," and not "tax evasion." What's the difference? $10,000 and prison time.

Never communicate with an IRS Special Agent without a reputable Criminal Tax Attorney speaking to the Agent on your behalf. And "never" means just that; Never.

**IRS Appeals Officer**

An IRS Appeals Officer is the IRS employee you meet when you file an IRS appeal of your tax audit. Whether you file an IRS Appeal with the IRS Office of Appeals, or with any Tax Court, you will meet with an IRS Appeals Officer.

Most IRS Appeals Officer were former IRS Tax Auditors or Revenue Agents whose work experience, knowledge of tax law, ability to resolve tax matters on agreed basis, and professional and personal commitment to the IRS, has elevated them up the employment ranks of the IRS. Appeals Officers are generally the most technically proficient and dedicated employees within the IRS. They are generally more casual and friendly and easy to deal with than IRS Tax Auditors and Revenue Agents.

Many Tax Professionals privately refer to the IRS Office of Appeals as the IRS "gift shop." Insider statistics reveal that an average IRS tax appeal results in almost a 50% decrease in a taxpayer's tax assessment. Those are good odds by anyone's playbook.

## IRS Attorney

An IRS attorney is the IRS employee you meet when you go to any U.S. Court that has jurisdiction over Federal tax matters. These courts are the U.S. Tax Court, U.S. Court of Appeals, U.S. District Court, and U.S. Bankruptcy Court. You will not meet an IRS Attorney when you go to an IRS office or field audit, or you go to the IRS Office of Appeals.

An IRS Attorney is employed by the Office of Chief Counsel for the IRS, located in Washington, D.C. The office of Chief Counsel is managed by the U.S. Department of Justice. Most IRS tax attorneys represent the IRS in tax civil litigation matters before the U.S. Tax Courts. The rest of the IRS Attorneys work in various other civil and criminal legal capacities, such as providing legal advisory services for Federal agencies, and prosecuting criminal cases on behalf of the U.S. Department of Justice.

## IRS Manager

All IRS employees have IRS Supervisors and IRS Managers that review their work and help resolve tax problems that arise between you and an IRS employee. You should ask to speak with a Supervisor or Manager in one or more of the following situations:

(1) You asked an impolite, rude, or hostile IRS auditor or agent to lighten up, and he or she refused to do so;

(2) You asked an IRS auditor or agent to recess the audit and schedule it on another day, because you became too upset during the audit, and he or she refused to do so; or

(3) You asked an IRS auditor or agent to recess the audit and schedule it on another day, because you needed to gather other supporting documents or discuss a tax law issue with your Tax Professional, and he or she refused to do so.

# CHAPTER 5

# IRS Tax Audit

Most people call them "Audits." The IRS prefers to call them "Examinations." Whatever people call them, they still involve the IRS trying to convince you to pay them more of your hard earned money.

Here is how the IRS defines an IRS Tax Audit:

"An IRS audit is a review and examination of an organization's or individual's accounts and financial information to ensure information is being reported correctly, according to the tax laws, to verify the amount of tax reported is accurate.

An audit may be conducted by mail or through an in-person interview and review of the taxpayer's records. The interview may be at an IRS office (office audit) or at the taxpayer's home, place of business, or accountant's office (field audit). The IRS will tell you what records are needed.

Audits can result in no changes or changes. Any proposed changes to your return will be explained."

IRS tax audits come in three delicious flavors: letter or computer correspondence; office; or field. Here is how the IRS views these tax audits:

An audit may be conducted by mail or through an in-person interview and review of the taxpayer's records. The interview may be at an IRS office (office audit) or at the taxpayer's home, place of business, or accountant's office (field audit). The IRS will tell you what records are needed. Audits can result in no changes or changes. Any proposed changes to your return will be explained."

An IRS tax audit can be concluded in one of three ways:

(1) No Change

A "No Change" audit involves an IRS tax audit in which you have substantiated all of the tax matters being reviewed, and your audit results in no changes.

(2) Agreed

An "Agreed" audit involves an IRS tax audit where the IRS proposes a tax change, and you understand and agree with the changes.

(3) Disagreed

A "Disagreed" audit involves an IRS tax audit where the IRS has proposed tax changes, and you understand the changes, but you disagree with the changes.

One interesting note. A Tax Professional who once worked for the IRS says that IRS auditors are praised and promoted by the "number" of audits completed during a tax year, and not by the "amount" of money collected during a tax year. Thank God.

## Statute of Limitations

The IRS has three years to start and end an audit of your Federal tax return.

In the event you file your tax return prior to April 15, the IRS has three years from April 15 to conclude your tax audit on your tax return. In the event you obtain an automatic extension from the IRS, and filed your tax return by October 15, the IRS has three years from October 15 to complete your tax audit.

If the IRS audited one of your Federal tax returns within the past two years, and you received a "no change" report or you paid the IRS no more than a $1000 in connection with your audit, and you receive another IRS tax audit request within the next two years, you should immediately contact the IRS and request a cancellation of the new audit. Go to the IRS Supervisor and Manager if necessary. This tax strategy can work, but not all the time. It's at least worth a good faith effort.

Like most laws, there always seems to be exceptions, and the three year statute of limitations has its exceptions. There are three situations where the IRS can audit your Federal tax return more than three years in the past:

(1) The IRS believes you underestimated your income on a tax return by 25% or more, in which case, the IRS has six years to start and end a tax audit;

(2) The IRS believes you filed a fraudulent tax return, in which case there is no statute of limitations for the IRS to start and end a tax audit; and

(3) You failed to file a tax return, in which case there is no statute of limitations for the IRS to start and end a tax audit.

**IRS Audit Rates**

Many business owners are curious about their chances of being selected for an IRS tax audit. You will be pleasantly surprised to know your chances are very minimal.

IRS audit rates fluctuate from year to year. Here are some general rules:

"Individual" audit rates fluctuate between 1 and 2%.

"Sole Proprietorship" audit rates fluctuate between 1% and 6%.

"S Corporation" audit rates fluctuate are less than 1% but are on the rise.

"C Corporation" audit rates are between 1% and 2%.

In summary, having only a 1-2% chance of being required to participate in some unwelcome experience is pretty reassuring odds.

## IRS Audit Selection

How the IRS selects tax returns for an IRS tax audit still remains a closely guarded secret by the IRS. Nevertheless, some secrets have leaked out to Tax Professionals. Just because you were selected for an IRS tax audit does not necessarily mean the IRS believes you owe more taxes. It may simply mean that the IRS wants to explore your tax return in greater depth with you. Yea, right!

Here is what the IRS says about how it selects people for an IRS tax audit:

"Selecting a return for audit does not always suggest that an error has been made. Returns are selected using a variety of methods, including random selection and computer screening - sometimes returns are selected based solely on a statistical formula. Document matching - when payor records, such as Forms W-2 or Form 1099, don't match the information reported. Related examinations - returns may be selected for audit when they involve issues or transactions with other taxpayers, such as business partners or investors, whose returns were selected for audit."

Warning! If you receive a telephone call from someone who claims to represent the IRS, ask for confirmation in writing. Never speak to this person before obtaining this written confirmation. If the person refuses to provide such confirmation, simply hang up your telephone. The IRS has a policy of first writing to you before calling you. In fact, the person on the telephone may be someone seeking free personal information about you. In other words, an Identity Thief. Beware.

Here are some of the potential reasons why you were chosen for an IRS tax audit:

(1) <u>Tax Return</u>

You didn't file a Federal income tax return.

(2) <u>IRS Computer</u>

The IRS computer selected you for a tax audit. More than one-half of all tax audits are triggered by the IRS National Computer Center, otherwise known as the "Discriminant Function" (DIF). Some of the reasons why the DIF chose your tax return include: your deductions are larger than similarly situated taxpayers; your deductions appear too large for your income; your deduction is out of character for your business; you reported a tax item in a wrong place on your tax return; you claim unusually large losses for your business; or you are a higher earning taxpayer.

(3) <u>IRS Market Segment Specialization Program</u>

The IRS Market Segment Specialization Program selected you for a tax audit. In such case, your business falls into a specific business industry or group whom the IRS believes has not fully complied with the tax laws. You may view these industries and groups in the IRS Audit Technique Guide that is published and made available to the public.

### (4) Local or National Tax Project

The IRS selected your tax return because of a local or national tax project involving certain businesses or occupations. This selection is similar to the IRS Market Segment Specialization Program but is implemented by human tax projects instead of the IRS computer.

### (5) Geographical Region

The IRS selected your tax return because you reside in a specific geographical region of the U.S.A. Some U.S. States have higher tax audit rates than other U.S. States. And no one other than the IRS seems to know why.

### (6) Amended Tax Return

The IRS selected your tax return because you filed an amended tax return, especially if you're amended tax return seeks a tax refund. Simply put, when you try to put the IRS into "Check," the IRS may try to put you into "Checkmate."

### (7) Criminal Matter

The IRS selected your tax return because you have been arrested, convicted, or are under investigation for an unrelated criminal matter, such as drug dealing, gambling, fraud, larceny, embezzlement, or other money related crimes.

### (8) Informant Tip

The IRS selected your tax return because of an informant's tip. Although difficult to believe, the IRS actually has a legal policy of paying people who rat you out to the IRS. The IRS pays informants a percentage of what the IRS collects. You can probably guess who these informants are. Here they are in order of popularity, from most popular to the least popular: Spouses, other family members, business partners, associates, and employees, disgruntled ex-girlfriend or ex-boyfriend, and neighbors. You will be wise to keep your friends close, and to keep your enemies even closer.

## Reducing IRS Audit Chances

As you can readily see from the forgoing discussion about IRS tax Audit Selection, there is not really much you can do about reducing your chances of an IRS tax audit. Well, maybe you can do real simple things like move to a more favorable U.S. State; change profession; under-report valid deductions; hide from your family; and not seek any tax refund. Yea, right. Even if you stop working and drop off the planet, the IRS can still audit you for failing to file a tax return.

The only realistic action you can take to reduce your chances of an IRS tax audit is to continue working hard at your business; implement all the tax reductions strategies learned in this study course; accept the remote possibility you will be selected for an IRS tax audit; and go to your IRS tax audit with a confident attitude that you will prevail.

As I have repeatedly advised you throughout this study course, the most important tax reduction strategy you can undertake to prevail at an IRS tax audit involves "audit proofing" your Federal tax returns. You must make it a routine habit to record and preserve your tax footprints by maintaining a daily log, regular file drawer, and permanent file cabinet.

Therefore, the key to audit proofing is "Documentation." Without proper documentation, you end up in the IRS tax cemetery where the IRS picks your bones clean. To avoid this tragedy, you must maintain written records that are accurate and complete, and which support your Federal income tax returns.

**IRS Audit Issues**

Most business owners are curious about what tax matters the IRS normally likes to audit. As I said at the beginning of this Chapter, "The more you know, the less you owe." Having a general knowledge about tax audit matters helps you stay confident.

Here are the top IRS audit issues, from most popular to least popular:

(1) Underreported Income

You failed to report all your 1099 income, W-2 wages, investment income, alimony, and retirement account withdrawals.

(2) Living Lavishly

You live lavishly and extravagantly, and well beyond your means, but you reported very little income for the year. The IRS uses four methods to determine your lifestyle:

(a) <u>Net Worth Method</u> - Your net worth has risen, but your reported income remains the same.

(b) <u>Expenditure Method</u> - Your annual expenditures exceed your annual income.

(c) <u>Bank Deposit Method</u> - Your annual bank deposits exceed your annual reported income.

(d) <u>Market Markup Method</u> - The IRS examines your annual business sales and annual expenses, and then determines that your annual profit exceeds your annual reported income. In such case, be ready to tell the IRS tax auditor about your savings accounts, trust fund accounts, disability payments, pensions, and financial assistance from family members.

## (3) Dependent Exemptions

You claim numerous individuals as dependents. In such case, be ready to show birth certificates and proof that family members are residing at your residential home. And your dependents better not have names like Fido and Fluffy and Rocky.

## (4) Medical Deductions

Your medical expenses are way out of proportion to your income. In such case, be ready to show the IRS your medical invoices and medical reports.

## (5) Charitable Deductions

Your charitable contributions are not in proportion to what similarly situated people contribute with the same income level. In such case, be ready to show the IRS written documentation of your charitable contribution. Remember, you must have receipts, regardless of the dollar amount, for all charitable contributions, and your contribution must go to a qualified charity, and not just for some good moral cause or needy family member or personal friend.

## (6) Travel and Entertainment Deductions

Your deductions are way out of proportion to your stated income, or lavish or extravagant. In such case, be ready to show written documentation.

## (7) Itemized Deductions

Your deductions appear overstated, lavish and extravagant, or are entered on the wrong line or wrong place on your tax return. Once again, be ready to show written documentation.

## (8) Unreimbursed Employee Business Expenses

Your deductions as an employee for travel, meals, lodging, entertainment, and home office appear overstated, lavish and extravagant, or are entered on the wrong line or the wrong place on your tax return. Be ready to show written documentation.

## (9) Tax Fraud

The IRS believes you have substantially underreported taxable income, and you have intentionally and repeatedly done so for several years. In such case, be ready to retain a criminal tax attorney! Just consider these beloved celebrities who the IRS went after for tax evasion: Martha Stewart, Wesley Snipes, Willie Nelson, Nicolas Cage, Richard Pryer, Sophia Loren, Heidi Fleiss, Marc Anthony, V.P. Spiro Agnew, Judy Garland, and Al Capone. And the list goes on and on and on.

**IRS Correspondence Audit**

An IRS Correspondence Audit begins when you receive a computer generated form from the IRS known as an IRS "Service Center Automatic Adjustment Notice." Technically speaking, this notice is not considered a tax audit by the IRS. The IRS calls it an "Adjustment Notice." Whatever the IRS calls it, it means the IRS wants more of your hard earned money.

Most IRS correspondence audits involve one or more of the following tax matters:

(1) Error Correction Notice

The IRS found some technical error or mathematical mistake on your tax return. You might have made a tax entry on the wrong line; or you listed three dependents, but only included the names of two dependents; or a mathematical calculation is incorrect.

(2) Unreported Notice

The IRS found a mismatch between two businesses. In other words, the IRS received one or more income reporting forms, such as a W-2, 1099, dividend, or retirement fund withdrawal, which you failed to report on your tax return.

(3) Interest Assessment Notice

The IRS believes you filed a correct tax return, but you did not make your tax payment in a timely manner. The IRS now wants you to pay interest for your error. For example, you underreported your Self-Employment taxes during the year.

(4) Penalty Assessment Notice

The IRS believes you filed a correct tax return, but you did not file your tax return in a timely manner. The IRS now wants you to pay interest for your error. For example, you filed your tax return after April 15 and before October 15, but you failed to obtain an IRS Form 4868 "Application for Automatic Extension of Time to File U.S. Individual Income Tax Return."

When you receive an IRS correspondence audit, you should always consider contesting the tax matter. If you can prove your tax return was correctly prepared, and you can provide supporting documents, you will prevail. It's that simple.

Here are the steps you should take when you receive an IRS correspondence audit:

(1) Consult a Tax Professional

You should first consult with a Tax Professional to determine the facts, law, and documents applicable to your

IRS tax matter. Most likely you can obtain proper tax guidance without having to hire a Tax Professional.

(2) Contact the IRS

After consulting with a Tax Professional, you or your Tax Professional should call the IRS, and explain your tax position. Immediately confirm your conversation with a letter restating your tax position with supporting documentation. If you have no supporting documentation, then consider paying the tax assessment.

Alternatively, instead of calling the IRS, send the IRS a letter, explaining your tax position, along with your supporting documents. If the IRS does not respond to your letter in a timely manner, but continues sending the same correspondence audit, send the IRS a copy of your original letter and documents. The IRS is very busy. It can take several weeks for the IRS to process your original letter. There is one time requirement you need to keep track of. You must contest any correspondence audit in writing within 60 days, or the tax adjustment becomes final.

(3) Petition U.S. Tax Court

Instead of calling or writing the IRS, you can simply ignore the IRS correspondence audit and wait for the IRS to send you a "Notice of Deficiency" letter. You then have 90 days to file a petition with the U.S Tax Court where you present you position and supporting documents before a Tax Court Judge.

**IRS Office Audit**

An IRS office Audit begins when you receive a computer generated letter from an IRS office Auditor. This letter normally includes the date, time, and IRS office location for your audit, or requests you to contact the IRS. The letter also includes the tax return being audited, and often an "information document request" which asks you to bring certain documents when you attend the audit.

An IRS office audit takes place at an IRS office. The IRS normally limits office audits to one to four tax matters, and the audit usually lasts between one to four hours. An IRS Tax Auditor will be attending the audit. As you can readily see, an IRS Office Audit is more expansive and can be more stressful than an IRS Correspondence Audit.

Here are the important steps you should take:

(1) Consult a Tax Professional

You should first consult with a Tax Professional to determine the facts, law, and documents applicable to your IRS tax matter. You should also decide if you want to retain the Tax Professional, or go to the audit with someone else, or go alone.

(2) Contact the IRS

Wait a short time after receiving the audit notice before you call the IRS Tax Auditor. You don't want to appear too anxious. Schedule the audit as far away into the future as possible; at the end of work week; and late in the month. Close to the audit date, if you are unable to roundup you're supporting documents, call the IRS Tax Auditor to reschedule the audit.

Alternatively, when you first contact the IRS Tax Auditor, ask the Auditor if the audit can be conducted by mail. In other words, try to change the audit from an office audit to a correspondence audit. You will need "good cause" for this request, such as an illness, disability, or long travel distance. There's no harm in asking.

(3) Prepare for the Audit

Once you schedule an audit date, gather your supporting documents, line up your witnesses, nail down the applicable facts and law, and clear your business calendar.

(4) Attend the Audit

When you attend the audit, wear clothes you normally wear to work, and arrive early. Only bring the relevant supporting documents, and not any additional documents, such as tax returns for prior and subsequent years.

Remain polite and cooperative, but not too cooperative. Talk as little as possible, and only about the relevant tax matter. If the IRS Tax Auditor asks you a "yes" or "no" question, obviously you should never say "yes" when the truth is "no." Instead, say something like: "I don't remember at the moment;" or "Give me some time to check on that;" or "Maybe my Tax-Pro knows the answer." Or simply look stupid while refusing to respond. As the Biblical goes: "Even a fool is thought wise when he keeps his mouth shut." Finally, if you're asked by the Tax

Auditor: "How hard are you working? How is business?" Simply reply: "Unbelievable. I work all day like a dog!" That will cover you whether business is good or bad.

You are legally permitted to tape record the audit. This can help guarantee a peaceful audit, and a formal record of what was said and done. It can also cause the auditor to become overly official and unwilling to negotiate. It's your decision. Just want you to know this option is available.

At the audit, you must prove your tax position with the facts, law, and substantial compliance. "Substantial Compliance" includes documents, photographs, computer generated materials, and your testimony. Just mention the "Cohan" rule if the IRS Tax Auditor balks at your tax deduction when you cannot produce any supporting documentation. The Auditor might raise his eyebrows, wondering how you knew about the Cohen rule. At the very least, you might score a couple tax points with the Auditor.

If the IRS Tax Auditor insists on supporting documents, and you're not sure you can locate the documents, say you will search for them, or simply refuse to provide the documents. Alternatively, instead of refusing to provide the documents, you might say something like: "I will look for them;" or "Let me first check with my Tax-Pro;" or if you really believe the documents have no relevance, politely refuse to comply.

In the event you fail to comply with the Auditor's document request, the Auditor basically has three choices:

First, the Auditor can obtain a court subpoena to serve upon you or another person or business. If you disobey the subpoena, the Auditor might force you to appear in front of a court judge who will decide the issue.

Second, the Auditor can search through voluminous IRS records retained all over the U.S.A., or records of other government and private agencies.

Finally, the Auditor might simply leave the issue alone, and move onto other tax matters, and then render a tax assessment without the documents.

One thing the Auditor will not do is attempt to legally enforce the "information document request" contained in your original IRS Tax Audit letter. This request carries no legal force in court.

## (5) Continuing a Tax Audit

You should request a continuance of the tax audit in any one of the following situations: First, you become too upset during the audit. Second, you need additional time to gather supporting documents or discuss a tax matter with your Tax Professional. Finally, the Auditor is impolite, rude, or hostile, and the IRS Tax Supervisor or Manager is not available. You're not a prisoner, even though you might feel like one. The Auditor has no inherent legal power to retain you. However, the Auditor can complete the audit and render an assessment without your further participation in the audit.

## IRS Field Audit

An IRS Field Audit begins when you receive a custom drafted letter from an IRS Revenue Agent. This letter normally includes the date, time, and IRS office location for the audit, or requests you to contact the IRS. The letter also includes the tax return(s) being audited, and often an "information document request" which identifies documents the Auditor wants to view.

An IRS office audit normally takes place at your place of business; or your tax representative's place of business; or your residential home. You can choose the location. The IRS Revenue Agent will go wherever you maintain your business and financial records.

A field audit usually involves a thorough examination of one or more Federal tax returns. The IRS Revenue Agent usually begins by conducting a one to two hour interview of you and your tax representative if you hired one. The entire field audit lasts anywhere from one day to several days, and sometimes even a week or more. As you can readily see, an IRS Field Audit is more expansive and stressful than an IRS office Audit or a correspondence audit.

Here is what the IRS says about a field audit for a charity or nonprofit organization. The same general conduct applies to any IRS field audit.

"In person *field* audits are conducted at (1) the organization's location, (2) the organization's representative's office or (3) a local IRS office. Generally, the audit will take place where the organization's books and records are located. Revenue agents should always identify themselves by presenting their official IRS pocket commissions (badges).

There are two kinds of field exams. The general program exam is typically conducted by a revenue agent who will visit the organization's location. The other type of field exam is called a Team Examination Program audit. This type of exam concerns large, complex organizations, and may involve a team of examiners."

All the audit strategies outlined in the previous section for an IRS Office Audit apply equally to an IRS Field Audit.

Here are additional recommendations that only apply to an IRS Field Audit:

First, do not let the IRS Revenue Agent talk with your staff, wander around the office, or make photocopies.

Second, if the Agent has a question, or wants to review a document, have the Agent put the request in writing, and then hand it to, or call, your Tax Professional, or deal with the issue yourself in a private location, such as your business office, if you have no Tax Professional.

Third, always remain physically present at your business office while the Agent is physically present at your office. Leaving the Agent alone at your office may encourage the Agent to wander around your office and talk with employees. You never want that to happen.

Finally, in the event you need to leave your office for business or personal reasons, politely ask the Agent to return again when you're available. An IRS Revenue Agent has no inherent legal authority to be inside your office without your express permission or a court order. If the Agent balks, simply shrug your shoulders, and say: "I'm sorry. But I have an important business matter I need to attend to."

**Concluding an IRS Office or Field Audit**

There comes a time when the IRS Tax Auditor or Revenue Agent wants to conclude your office or field audit and issue you an IRS "Examination Report." The Examination Report explains the proposed tax liability, interest, and penalties. You can expect to be told one of two things: no change, or you owe more taxes.

This is a very special moment, for it provides you with another opportunity to stand up for your legal rights. You must remain calm and under total control of your mental and physical facilities. Will standing up for your tax rights result in a larger tax assessment? You might naturally think so, but just the opposite is generally true. The more work you make for an Auditor or Agent, the more they want to conclude the audit and move onto a more timid and easier victim.

Here are the important steps you should take when you're Auditor or Agent wants to conclude your tax audit:

### (1) Stay Confident and Curious

Questions don't constitute admissions, only statements do. So don't be shy about having the Auditor or Agent answer your questions, or the legal basis for a proposed tax assessment, or a detailed explanation of what adjustments are included in the Examination Report. If you decide to raise the bar, and go on the attack, just make certain to remain focused on attacking a particular tax matter, and not on attacking the Auditor or Agent personally. This is one of the cardinal rules of professional negotiators and mediators: always "separate the problem from the people." For example, no hard-biting IRS jokes. Never say: "I don't know if I can live within my income or not; you IRS guys won't let me try it."

### (2) Extend the Audit

If you don't like what you hear from the Auditor or Agent, simply ask for more time to retrieve documents; more time to consult with your Tax Professional; or more time to gather your faculties when you're too upset to think and act rationally.

### (3) Point Out Favorable Deductions

If you do not require any more time, this is the perfect moment to take the offensive. Begin by pointing out any additional tax deductions, adjustments, and credits you're entitled to on your tax return. Don't reveal these tax matters prior to this moment. Otherwise, you might cause the Auditor or Agent to dig deeper for something, and you don't want that to happen. You'll also gain more negotiation leverage by waiting until now to disclose tax matters beneficial to you.

## (4) Negotiate a Compromise

Always try to present factual and legal tax positions and proposals in a language the IRS understands and accepts. For example, don't speak dollars. Speak percentages. In other words, don't say: "Can we agree upon 50 cents on the dollar for my doctor bills?" Instead, say: "Can we agree upon a 50% compromise for my medical deduction?"

Here are some general negotiation tools recommended by negotiation professionals. Separate the people from the problem. Focus on interests, not positions. Invent options for mutual gain. Insist on using objective criteria. In a nutshell, attempt to negotiate a "Win-Win" situation for both you and the IRS.

## (5) Extending the Audit

If the Auditor or Agent asks you to extend the audit beyond the three year statute of limitation, you should consider accepting the request, but limiting the extension to six months, and only for specific tax matters.

## (6) Receipt of Examination Report

Upon receipt of the Examination Report that proposes additional taxes, you have several viable options:

You can sign the Examination Report. This doesn't mean you immediately agree to pay the proposed tax liability. Instead, you can sign an IRS "Installment Agreement," or consider an IRS "Offer in Compromise." However, an Offer in Compromise is normally limited to destitute individuals who have little or no assets.

Alternatively, you can refuse to sign the Examination Report, contact an IRS Manager, and resume negotiations with the manager.

Finally, you can simply ignore the Examination Report, in which case, the IRS will send you a "30 Day Letter," at which time, you can file an appeal with the IRS Office of Appeals or the U.S. Court system.

# CHAPTER 6

# IRS Tax Appeal

The IRS will not guarantee you an automatic right to an administrative appeal before the IRS Office of Appeals. Fortunately, Federal law does guarantee you a legal right to a judicial appeal to a U.S. Court.

Even if you do not have a legal right to appeal your case to the IRS Office of Appeals, the IRS routinely grants such requests.

Here is what the IRS says about its Office of Appeals:

"Every year, the IRS Office of Appeals helps over 100,000 taxpayers resolve their tax disputes without going to Tax Court. We are an independent organization within the IRS whose mission is to help taxpayers and the government resolve tax disagreements. The Office of Appeals does not take sides in a dispute; rather we offer an objective point of view on each individual case.

Appeals also offers mediation services through Fast Track Settlement, Early Referral, and other mediation programs. These mediation programs are designed to help you resolve your dispute at the earliest possible stage in the audit or collection process.

Appeals is the place for you if all of the following apply: You received a letter from the IRS explaining your right to appeal the IRS's decision. You do not agree with the IRS's decision. You are not signing an agreement form sent to you."

There are three good reasons for requesting an appeal with the IRS Office of Appeals: First, an appeal is very simple, and there are no administrative costs. Second, an appeal results in some tax savings almost 50% of the time. Finally, an appeal delays your tax bill.

**IRS Office of Appeals**

Here is how to file an Appeal with the IRS Office of Appeals:

(1) <u>IRS 30 Day Letter</u>

When you receive the IRS "30 day letter," file your appeal by certified mail with the IRS Office of Appeal within 30 days of the date of the IRS letter. If your tax matter is less than $25,000, file a form entitled "Request for Appeals Review." If your tax matter exceeds $25,000, file a formal protest letter. You can ask for an extension of time to file an appeal from the IRS Auditor, Agent, or Manager, but make certain to obtain their express consent in writing.

## (2) Appeals Conference

An IRS Appeals hearing can be conducted by mail, correspondence, or in person. All the recommendations made regarding an IRS office and field audit apply equally to an IRS appeals conference. In the event you attend a face-to-face appeal hearing, your meeting will take place with an IRS Appeals Officer in a private office in an informal setting.

Just like an IRS office audit, you are legally permitted to tape record the Appeals conference. This can ensure a formal record of what was said and done. And also like an IRS office audit, your recording may cause the Appeals Officer to become overly official and stifle the negotiation process. It's your call.

## (3) Negotiate a Compromise

Just like that special moment when your IRS Auditor or Agent wanted to close out your case, when you're at the appeals conference, try to negotiate a final settlement that involves a "win-win" deal for both parties.

First, ask to have the interest and penalties removed.

Next, ask for a reduction in your tax liability by speaking the IRS talk and walking the IRS walk. In other words, talk the IRS language. Use Percentages, not dollars. Discuss deductions, adjustments, credits; not "my kids" or "my gasoline bill." Accept some adjustments, unless they are entirely wrong. Stay focused on the tax matter and avoid making any personal attacks on the tax auditor or agent. Be realistic and flexible. Weigh the cost of litigation.

Get creative. Most importantly, ask for additional time to consult with your Tax Professional if you are unsure about something.

(4) <u>Settlement</u>

If you successfully achieve a final compromise, you will be signing an IRS settlement form called a "Consent to Proposed Tax Adjustment."

(5) <u>Appeal</u>

If you're unable to reach a final compromise of your tax matter with the IRS Appeals Officer, you still have the legal option of continuing your tax case in one of several U.S. Courts. When you fail to reach a settlement, you will receive an IRS "Notice of Deficiency" letter, otherwise known as a "90 Day Letter." This letter starts the clock ticking for filing your appeal with a U.S. Court. If you ignore this letter, your tax liability will become final with no more avenues of adjudication.

**U.S. Courts**

You should consider a U.S. Court whenever you feel confident about your tax position; you're not pleased with the results of the tax audit; and you have been unable to reach a final compromise in the IRS Office of Appeals.

You can file your appeal in one of several U.S. Court. There are advantages and disadvantages with each court. For example, the U.S. Tax Court does not require you to pay the assessed tax before your court hearing, but the U.S District Court has this legal requirement. Also, in the U.S.

Tax Court, a judge will decide your case at an informal trial, as compared to the U.S. District Court where you can choose between a judge trial and a jury trial.

Even if you decide to file an appeal, you still have plenty of time and opportunities to continue with meaningful settlement negotiations before your day in court. In fact, if you choose to go to the U.S. Tax Court, you will be required to return to the IRS Office of Appeals for another round of settlement negotiation before your trial date. You get two bites of the apple.

## U.S. Tax Court

The United States Tax Court is a Federal Trial Court of record established by Congress under Section 8 of Article I of the U.S. Constitution, which provides that Congress has the power to "constitute tribunals inferior to the supreme Court." The U.S Tax Court is located in Washington, D.C.

### Court Website

You can find the U.S. Tax Court at ustaxcourt.gov. At the Court website, you can view the rules of practice and procedures, fees, court forms, the Judges' biographies, the court docket, current and former court opinions, and even Court press releases.

### Court Procedures

Once the IRS has sent you a "Notice of Deficiency" letter, otherwise known as a "90 Day Letter," advising you of your tax liability, you can dispute the deficiency in the U.S. Tax Court before paying the disputed amount.

Besides tax matters, the U.S. Tax Court has legal jurisdiction to redetermine transferee liability, make certain types of declaratory judgments, adjust partnership items, order abatement of interest, award administrative and litigation costs, redetermine worker classification, determine relief from joint and several liability on a joint return, review certain collection actions, and review awards to whistleblowers who provide information to the IRS.

The U.S. Tax Court is composed of more than one dozen presidential appointed Judges. Your tax matter will be decided by one of these Judges without a jury trial. Although the U.S. Tax Court is physically located in Washington, D.C., the Trial Judges travel nationwide to conduct trials in various cities located in all 50 U.S. States.

A U.S. Tax Court case commences when you file a "Petition." Your petition must be filed within 90 days of the date of IRS Notice of Deficiency letter. The U.S. Tax Court cannot extend the time for filing your petition. Upon filing your petition, payment of your proposed tax assessment is postponed until your case has been decided by the Trial Judge.

In U.S. Tax Court disputes involving $50,000 or less, you may elect to have your case conducted under the Court's simplified small tax case procedure, otherwise known as the "S" Court. Trials in the small Tax Court cases generally are less formal and result in a speedier disposition. In fact, these trials are very similar to the informal trials conducted in your local Civil Small Claims Court. The Tax Judge's decision in a small Tax Court case will be final, and you therefore have no right to any appeal of your case to another court. In contrast, trials conducted in the regular U.S. Tax Court follow strict rules of legal procedure and evidence, and the Judge's decision is appealable. The Trial Judges are generally less patient with taxpayers who represent themselves "in pro per."

Upon filing your petition, the U.S. Tax Court will "calendar" your case for a trial. You will be notified by the court of the date, time, and place of trial. Trials are conducted before one judge, without a jury, and you may be represented by any attorney admitted to practice before the Tax Court. You may also represent yourself "in pro per" if you desire.

You will receive three written notices from the U.S. Tax Court prior to your trial date:

(1) Notice Setting Case for Trial

The Trial Judge assigned to your case will send you a court notice, advising you of the date, time, and place you case is set for trial. If your tax audit involved a marital joint tax return, only you or your spouse needs to attend the court trial.

The initial date scheduled by the Trial Judge may actually involve a "Calendar Call" date which will not be the actual trial date. If your case includes a Calendar Call, you must appear on this date. The Judge will ask you and the IRS Trial Attorney if your both ready for trial, and if both of you answer "yes," the Judge will set an actual trial date in the very near future, normally within a week.

If you live far from the U.S. Tax Court, call the Clerk of the Court a week prior to your initial Court date, and ask for permission to attend the Calendar Call by telephone. Most Judges will grant your request.

(2) Standing Pre-Trial Order

The Trial Judge assigned to your case will order you and the IRS Trial Attorney to attend a settlement conference before your trial date. The IRS Attorney will contact you to determine an agreed date, time, and place for the settlement conference.

The settlement conference is normally scheduled at least 30 days prior to your trial date. If you reach a final resolution of your tax matter at the settlement conference, the IRS attorney will prepare a settlement document called a "Stipulated Tax Court Decision" for your signature.

If you are unable to reach a final settlement, you and the IRS Attorney must prepare a joint written stipulation of facts, and also exchange a written list of witnesses who may testify at your trial.

(3) Trial Memorandum

The Trial Judge assigned to your case will order you and the IRS Trial Attorney to each prepare a separate written Trial Memorandum. Your memorandum will include a factual summary; the tax issues; the disputed tax amount; the names of your witnesses and what they intend to say; legal authorities; any evidentiary issues; an estimate of how long your trial will last; and whether you wish to discuss your case with a settlement judge prior to the trial. If you represent yourself "in pro per," don't be intimidated by this memorandum. Judges don't expect much from individual's representing themselves before the Tax Court.

## (4) Court Trial

Your Court Trial will be open to the general public, so feel free to bring anyone you like along with you for moral support. A small Tax Court case will normally last no longer than two hours. Simply present your case like you would in a Civil Small Claims Court.

Following your trial, the Judge will issue a written report setting forth findings of fact, along with a judicial opinion. Do not expect to receive this report for at least one month. The Judge will then close your case by entering a decision with the Court.

If you win your case in the U.S. Tax Court, and you retained an attorney to represent you, you can ask the Trial Judge to award you "Litigation and Administrative Costs" for your attorney fees and certain court costs. To prevail, you must show you were the prevailing party at trial, and the IRS position was not legally justified. In other words, you must convince the Trial Judge that the IRS was dead wrong, and the IRS knew or should have known it was dead wrong all along.

(5) Appeal Rights

If you do not win your case in the U.S Tax Court, and your case involves an "S" case, you have no further appellate rights. Your case has reached a final judgment.

If your case was heard in the Regular Tax Court, you must submit a formal legal brief to the Trial Judge after your Court trial. You can then file an appeal to a U.S Court of Appeals, and if you don't like the decision there, you can file a final discretionary appeal to the U.S. Supreme Court.

## U.S. Court of Federal Claims

Instead of filing an appeal of an IRS tax assessment in the U.S. Tax Court, you can file an appeal in the U.S Court of Federal Claims.

This Court is authorized primarily to hear money disputes founded upon the U.S. Constitution, Federal Statutes, executive regulations, and contracts. Many cases before the U.S. Court of Federal Claims involve tax refund lawsuits. These cases generally involved complex factual and legal issues regarding tax laws. The court is located in Washington, D.C. You can view information about this Court at uscourts.gov.

The Judges in the U.S. Court of Federal Claims are stricter, and the rules of civil procedure are more meticulously as compared to the U.S. Tax Court. The Judges are also less friendly to taxpayers representing themselves "in pro per." You can choose to have a Judge Trial or a Jury Trial.

To file an appeal, you must first wait for the IRS to send you an IRS 90 day Notice of Deficiency letter. You then file an IRS "Claim for Refund," along with payment of the IRS tax assessment, and wait for the IRS to officially deny your refund claim. Your appeal in the U.S. Court of Federal Claims then becomes a claim for a refund of overpaid taxes.

If you are dissatisfied with the decision of the U.S. Court of Federal Claims, you can file an Appeal with a U.S Court of Appeals, and if you're still dissatisfied, you can file a final discretionary appeal to the U.S Supreme Court.

## U.S. District Court

Instead of filing an appeal of an IRS tax assessment with the U.S. Tax Court or the U.S. Court of Federal Claims, you can file an Appeal in a U.S District Court.

U.S. District Courts are authorized to adjudicate a wide variety of civil and criminal matters. Only a small number of cases before the Court involve tax refund lawsuits. Most tax cases before the U.S. District Court involve complex factual and legal issues regarding tax laws. U.S District Courts are located all across the U.S. States. You can view information about your local U.S. District Court by going online and typing "U.S. District Court," along with the name of your city.

On the positive side, you can choose a Judge Trial or a Jury Trial in the U.S. District Court.

On the negative side, like the U.S. Court of Federal Claims, you must pay the IRS tax assessment before you can file a Petition with the U.S. District Court. Also, be forewarned. You will be eaten alive by the judge if you handle your tax matter alone "in pro per." The Judges in the U.S. District Court are even more strict than the Judges in the U.S. Court of Federal Claims, and they have absolutely no patience for any taxpayer who is not well versed in the rules of civil procedure. You certainly want a competent tax attorney representing you in the U.S. District Court.

To file an appeal, you must first wait for the IRS to send you an IRS 90 day Notice of Deficiency. You then file an IRS "Claim for Refund," along with payment of the full tax assessment, and wait for the IRS to officially deny your refund claim. Your clam in the U.S. District Court then becomes a claim for a refund of overpaid taxes.

You can appeal a U.S. District Court decision to a U.S Court of Appeals, and if you're dissatisfied with the decision, you can file a final discretionary appeal with the U.S Supreme Court.

## U.S. Bankruptcy Court

Hopefully, you are a successful business owner who is not a serious candidate for bankruptcy. However, it's always good to know that a Bankruptcy Court is available to hear and decide your IRS tax case if you fall into financial trouble, and also have a serious tax issue pending before the IRS. Bankruptcy Courts have made tax rulings very favorable to U.S. Taxpayers. And best of all, you don't have to pay your IRS tax assessment before going there.

# Other Books by
# Brent J. Jordan, Esq., LL.M.

Kill Your Taxes Dead

10 Powerful Tax Strategies that Pass IRS Scrutiny

Automatic Millionaire: Financial Independence for Young People

Create a Happy Lifestyle in One Day

Live 1,000 Years

J4RD4N:
A Mind Bending, Gut Wrenching, Miracle Infused, Life Journey

Learning to Breathe

6 Supercharged Stories